ME X ICO
PAINTER & ARTISAN

November 21, 1995 - February 28, 1996
Washington D.C. - U.S.A.
Mexican Cultural Institute

contemporary art

mexican popular art

PULSAR INTERNACIONAL, S.A. DE C.V.
Wishes to express its appreciation to the following individuals
and organizations for their cooperation:

THE EMBASSY OF MEXICO IN THE WASHINGTON, D.C.

THE HONORABLE JESUS SILVA HEZOG
Ambassador to the U.S.A.

MEXICAN CULTURAL INSTITUTE

D. MANUEL COSIO
General Director

MS. ELENA GUAJARDO DE KIMBERLY
CHAIRPERSON OF THE BOARD OF PATRONS

VIVA

ADVERTISING AND PUBLIC RELATIONS
MR. MICHAEL, DIESTE
DALLAS, TEXAS

COPYRIGHT © 1995 BY PULSAR INTERNACIONAL, S.A. DE C.V.
EDIFICIO TORREALTA. AV. ROBLE NO. 900, MEZZANIME
COL. VALLE DEL CAMPESTRE
66265 SAN PEDRO GARZA GARCIA
NUEVO LEON, MEXICO
FAX (52-8) 356 7332

D.L. M-17.433-1995
I.S.B.N. 84-605-3059-0

PRINTED IN SPAIN

ARTISTIC PATRIMONY

WITH THE COLLECTIONS

FEBRES

AND THE COLLABORATION

Mexican Embassy

MEXICAN CULTURAL INSTITUTE

Table of contents

	Page
Presentation by the Chairman of the board of Directors and Executive President of Pulsar Internacional Alfonso Romo Garza	5
Message of the Ambassador of Mexico to the United States of America The honorable Jesús Silva-Herzog	6
Message of the General Director of the Mexican Cultural Institute Manuel Cosío	7
Contemporary Art by Consuelo Fernández Ruiz	8
Biographies of the Artists and Photographs of the Contemporary Art Paintings Art Collection of "Seguros Comercial America"	10
Mexican Folk Art by María Esther Echeverría Zuno	80
Photographs of the Mexican Folk Art Pieces Collection of "Cigarrera La Moderna"	82
List of Photographic Illustrations	145

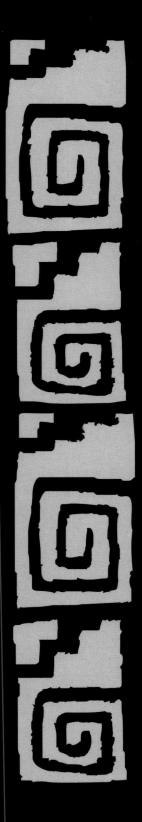

PULSAR
Pulsar International

It is indeed a great satisfaction to present to the U.S. Community, and particularly to the City of Washington, D.C., the eshibition: Mexico Pictorial and Folk Art.

This satisfaction comes from being able to present the traditions, customs and values of Mexico in the eshibition halls of the Mexican Cultural Institute, a task in which the involvement of the Ministry of Culture and the cooperation of the Embassy of Mexico in the United States of America have been vital.

The exhibition presents 201 Mexican folk art pieces and 68 oil paintings by renowned Mexican artists.

All of these works are part of the Cultural Heritage of Pulsar and come from the collections of our companies La Moderna, and Seguros Comercial America, and have already been displayed in Holland, Canada, Spain and other countries.

Pulsar would like to express its deep appreciation for having been invited by the Mexican Cultural Institute to exhibit these works.

Alfonso Romo Garza
Chairman of the Board of Directors
and Executive President of Pulsar International

5

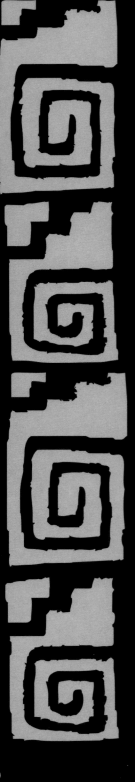

Mexican Embassy

In keeping with Mexico's endeavor to promote and enhance the beauty of its culture and maintaining the belief that cooperative effort is the foundation for every success, PULSAR, S.A. and The Mexican Cultural Institute have brought the impressive collection of masterpieces «Mexico: Painter and Artisan» to the cities of Dallas and Washington, D.C.

This collection, whose artists were inspired by an affinity with their magnificent surroundings, a dedication to personal consciousness and an expression of the bond with Mexico's past, represents the universality of the Mexican spirit and its zeal to express itself through art.

I would like to thank the organizers of this exhibition for their repeated efforts which have been carried out with dedication and excellence. Exhibits such as these are testmony to both the grandeur of a country's culture and its willingness to share it with the American people.

Jesús Silva-Herzog F.
Ambassador of Mexico

MEXICAN CULTURAL INSTITUTE

The exhibit «Mexico: Painter and Artisan», sponsored by Grupo Pulsar Internacional, S.A. de C.V. presented at the Central Civic Park of Dallas, Texas and The Mexican Cultural Institute of Washington D.C., is without a doubt one of the finest examples of the great heights reached by Mexican art in this Century.

The painter's names are proof enough of the importance of this exhibit. The quality of work presented here and stylistic diversity give this show a panoramic vision of Mexican contemporary art.

On the other hand, the magnificent handicrafts, which combine their intrinsic qualities with the pictoric collection, make this exhibit unique inasmuch as they show the continuing dialogue between popular art and the so called serious or academic school.

This is the second occasion that Grupo Pulsar, S.A. de C.V. sponsors an important exhibition in the United States, proving its dedication to promote the knowledge of Mexican art in this country.

On behalf of The Mexican Cultural Institute. I wish to express our gratitude for giving us the opportunity to promote the best of Mexican art and handicrafts during a time in which the preservation of cultural roots, the essence our identity as a nation, is of such great importance.

Manuel Cosío
Minister for Cultural Affairs and
Director of the Mexican Cultural Institute
in Washington D.C.

7

popular art

Pulsar International has undertaken, in conjunction with its mass production, the promotion of our culture through the acquisition of important pieces of Mexican Art. Pulsar, aware of the fact that enhancement and progress are fundamentally based on the talent and innovative capacity of the artist and businessman, presents a sample of the creativity of the Mexican artist.

This goal has allowed the institution to acquire a collection of paintings in which we find multiple and dynamic interpretations of our history, of our recent past and of a future that is being written, while finding in art a multifaceted picture of individual visions, collective feelings and fantasies.

Each work has specific value. The theme which inspires them is the presentation of our country through the circumstances, capabilities and motivations of the artists, within their individual historic framework.

The new artistic expressions that developed at the end of the XIXc. and the first two decades of our century may be found in modernism. Among its representatives we find: Saturnino Herrán, forerunner of synthesism, expressive art, heartfelt Mexican paintings; Joaquín Clausell who brought impressionism from Paris adopting it in order to offer a personal interpretation of the Mexican landscape; Gerardo Murillo, "Dr. Atl", painter, volcanoist and writer, known for his landscapes of volcanoes painted with self-invented techniques.

Later on, culture and its various expressions becomes part of the new Mexico. In search of self-definition, the mural becomes one of the most authentic pictoric movements with profound social content: Diego Rivera, José Clemente Orozco and David Alfaro Siqueiros had different styles and personalities when painting murals or working at the easel.

In the second stage of muralism, oustanding muralists such as Juan O'Gorman, Pablo O'Higgins, Roberto Montenegro and José Chávez Morado came to the forefront. During those times other gifted painters like Frida Kahlo, (accepted in the Mexican ambience even though she departs from the forms that were the status quo of the "Mexican School"), María Izquierdo who paints with freedom of expression and spontaneity; Federico Cantú, painter that also developes muralism using predominantly religious themes.

During the 50's a group of artists appeared that cried out for expression that would be both subjective and free from content, a counter-position of the social and political ideals that inspired muralism. The most widely known artists are: Pedro and Rafael Coronel whose passionate interests were to capture, interpret and transmit our artistic pre-hispanic heritage and the obsession of placing their work under constant and rigorous review with that of the western world; and Gunther Gerzo with a repertoire mostly made by intellectual geometric structures, almost always asymetric.

Consuelo Fernández Ruíz

Herrán does not travel to Europe; he doesn't have highs or lows in his life; rather he concentrates on his vocation while struggling against economic adversities.

He transforms everything into a very personal and Mexican language; he knew how to transform himself and his painting and he distanced himself from strict academic tradition and romantic themes.

He possesed a rare sincerity and he was free of racial and social prejudices. For Saturnino Herrán an aesthetic interpretation of Mexican life means moving towards a profound and broad understanding of our being. What interests him is all that is alive, the human cultural *mestizaje* and that we are the result of a remote indigenous past. We can see an example of this in his "Self-portrait", since like most Mexicans, both cultures are reflected in him.

"Old Man's Head" is a work in which he manipulates with great narrative intensity the light and shadows, the perfection of the line which shows the looseness of the skin, the melancholy expression of the stare and the austerity of the background. All these elements are brought together to convey a profound loneliness to the spectator. The brush strokes are broad and pasty and the abundance of color media used is adopted from Impressionism.

The sketch "The Offering" depicts an Indian family wandering on the path of their tragedy, in the morning mist, carrying to the market the mournful "zempoaxochitl", the flower of the dead. The Indians are wearing the traditional clothing and their bronze faces harmonize with the yellow tones of the flowers. The forms are presented synthetically and decoratively. In the painting, Herrán shows us that the world of the common people, the humble, what the Europeanized would consider vulgar, is a noble world full of profound and sincere emotions.

There is a line from the celebrated writer Justo Sierra that is very closely associated with the thought of Saturnino Herrán:

"We Mexicans are the children of two peoples and of two races; we were born of the conquest: our roots are in the land inhabited by the aboriginal peoples and on Spanish soil. This fact dominates our entire history: to it we owe our soul."

Saturnino Herrán

(Aguascalientes, Ags. 1888 - Mexico City 1918)

It is in Aguascalientes, his birthplace, that he begins his first studies and his vocation emerges. At 14, due to his father's death, he moves with his family to the capital and two years later he enters the School of Fine Arts.

Antonio Fabrés, the last European teacher hired by the government to come to the San Carlos Academy, known at that time as the School of Fine Arts, is the one who discovers his talent considering him his favorite student.

1

SATURNINO HERRÁN
Self-portrait
Autorretrato
undated / *sin fecha*
oil on canvas / *óleo sobre tela*

2

SATURNINO HERRÁN
Old Man's Head
Cabeza de viejo
undated / *sin fecha*
oil on canvas / *óleo sobre tela*

3

SATURNINO HERRÁN
The Offering
La ofrenda
undated / *sin fecha*
pencil on paper / *lápiz sobre papel*

13

Francisco Goitia

(Patillos, Zacatecas 1882 - Mexico City 1960)

A disciple of the great landscape painter José María Velasco, of the visionary Julio Ruelas, of the rigorous academic Germán Gedovius and of the nationalist, Saturnino Herrán.

He travels to Barcelona, Spain, and there he studies with Francisco Galli, staying in Europe until 1912. Upon returning to Mexico, he joins the ranks of the villistas dedicating himself to the cause of the indigenous people, acting as a teacher and rural advocate. At the end of his life he renounces all material goods and he lives in a small hut in Xochimilco, channeling his efforts towards social service carried out as a loyal follower of the Franciscan order.

The composition "Self-portrait" is based on the superimposition of diversely textured, broad chromatic fields, which shape his work. The weak torso is emphasized by the enormous scale of the strong hands that support the palette and the brush.

Goitia pays more attention to the face, emerging from tonal and chromatic variations that emphasize every trait, every line, every light and every shadow, each having its own value and content.

4

FRANCISCO GOITIA
Self-portrait
Autorretrato
undated / *sin fecha*
oil on canvas / *óleo sobre tela*

00In Impressionism it is no longer a matter of painting objects, but the shifting light reflected on them, creating a visual effect whose image should be captured and expressed in an impressionistic way. In other words, by a free and bold technique capable of transmitting to the spectator the impression and the effect captured by the painter's eye and his sensibility. From there the need arose to juxtapose the brush strokes of various tones in order to give the visual illusion of the luminosity of the object, not the object itself, but a whole new world of appearances. In terms of topics, they were no longer historic places but any place that was important for the painter: a street, a field of colors, a place in the park or the woods at whatever time of day.

At the age of twenty Clausell moves to the capital where, in 1896, he earns a law degree, although two years earlier he went to Europe for political reasons. Being of revolutionary ideas, a friend of truth and justice, he consequently went to jail several times.

Orozco, who encouraged Clausell to paint, said: "he carried in his hands the rainbow of the impressionists and all the boldness of the Paris school."

Most of his works are not signed or dated. He was self-taught and sold on the formal principles put forth by Impressionism, adopting them to bring a more personal interpretation to the Mexican landscape. His impressionism is not as brilliant and subtle as that of the French painters; his colors are rich but harsh; his forms are strong. His heavy-handedness is, as Justino Fernández would say: "very virile art, but not exempt from sentimental delicacy."

Besides his landscapes, Clausell leaves in his study, in the house where he lived (the old mansion of the Count and Countess of Santiago de Calimaya, today the Museum of Mexico City), the walls painted with small sketches of naked human figures and dreams. It is there that he shaped his fantasy and part of his biography.

The painting "Seascape" includes the use of some mixed-media techniques: the noticeable handling of a spatula, detailed and superimposed pastings to give texture to the rocks and thin rubbings to represent the sky and clouds, extending to the outlining of the coasts by use of large successive strokes.

Joaquín Clausel

1 (Campeche 1866 - Mexico City 1935)

In the last quarter of the 19th century Impressionism was being developed in France as the latest form of artistic expression. In Mexico impressionist painting was not truly a movement. Other horizons were being sought in art. Among them, the very personal impressionism of Joaquín Clausell, an artist who takes new steps in landscape painting.

16

5

JOAQUÍN CLAUSELL
Seascape
Marina
undated / *sin fecha*
oil on canvas / *óleo sobre tela*

17

Rosario Cabrera

(1900-1975)

From the time she was a small girl she showed an inclination for painting. Her first step towards an artistic education is at the "Open-Air School" (directed by Alfredo Ramos Martínez). This is the beginning of a significant movement in which the objective is to awaken an appreciation for the beauty of our country and to give birth to a truly national art; to have direct contact with nature; removing the students from the dark classrooms of the Academy. As such the students go out, guided by a teacher, to the countryside, or they sat in the plazas or streets of small villages or they went into abandoned gardens to capture the light and various changes with their artistic materials.

Along with her artistic work Rosario Cabrera also becomes a teacher. She goes on to teach many generations, demanding integrity in the education of the young people in the teaching profession in Mexico.

"Girl with a Pink Ribbon" is a portrait from her youth in which she reveals great agility with the brush and a command of color.

The work "The Green-Eyed Lady" is influenced somewhat by Ramos Martínez and shows a certain affectation and a distant abandon of the model.

The lady dresses and wears her hair in the style that in the 1930's served as a source of humor or as a joke among the people of the small towns. The hair style, referred to at that time with the French term "a la garconne", emulated the style worn by young men, inspiring ballads that soon spread throughout the country:
> "no more crew-cuts
> no more pretense
> Whoever wants to be bald
> will pay a tax".

The make-up used during that period minimized the tan face of the Mexican woman by its paleness and the darkness of the shadows. Her thick lips were made thin with small bits of red lipstick. The ivory paleness has a counterpart in the whiteness of the dress falling smoothly from the shoulders.

6

ROSARIO CABRERA
The Girl with Pink Ribbon
La niña con moño rosa
undated / *sin fecha*
oil on canvas / *óleo sobre tela*

ROSARIO CABRERA
The Green-Eyed Lady
La dama de los ojos verdes
undated / *sin fecha*
oil on canvas / *óleo sobre tela*

Gerardo Murillo, "Dr. Atl"

(Guadalajara, Jalisco 1875 - Mexico City 1964)

Painter, volcanologist, writer, and a man of violent reactions. A restless spirit, he had many diverse interests in his life: science, politics and art. He was among the first to pay attention to popular art and to dedicate his efforts to learning about it, both promoting and collecting it.

His profession as a painter begins in Guadalajara and continues in the Academy of San Carlos. When he was twenty-one he traveled to Europe where he studied philosophy and volcanology in Rome.

There are various stories as to how he got his pseudonym "Dr. Atl", an Aztec sound meaning "water". The first is that it was the Argentine poet Leopoldo Lugones who baptized him as such, and the second is that Gerardo Murillo gave him that name due to the fact that he was against anything Spanish.

Together with Diego Rivera, José Clemente Orozco and Siqueiros, he is among the great innovators in Mexican painting. Dr. Atl is known for his landscapes and for his favorite theme: the volcano.

Such is the case in his works "Volcanoes and Horizons" and "Popocatepetl Volcano" in which one can appreciate the curvilinear perspective, the precision of his drawing, which allows simplified forms and details, and lastly the bright colors generated by the "Atl colors" - paints which he himself invented by mixing a hard paint made of wax, resin and oil. Like pastels, these paints can be used on any surface. The shades can be layered indefinitely while remaining pure, but not blending. The paintings done with this material have both a matte and shiny finish.

In later years he flies over volcanoes, painting them, and as such he creates a new genre called "aeropainting", in which he aims to visually capture vast extensions of land.

8

GERARDO MURILLO
"DR. ATL"
Volcanoes and Horizons
Volcanes y horizontes
1935
mixed media on playwood /
técnica mixta sobre triplay

9

**GERARDO MURILLO
"DR. ATL"**
The Popocatepetl Volcano
El Volcan Popocatepetl
1947
mixed media on dry-mounting /
técnica mixta sobre fibracel

Diego Rivera

(Guanajuato,Gto. 1886 - Mexico City 1957)

His training as a painter begins at the Academy, but soon he rebels against the teachings of Antonio Fabrés. In 1907 he goes off to Europe where he stays until 1921. This trip opens up many new possibilities and there he witnesses the development of Fauvism and Cubism, and makes his first important contribution to contemporary art along side Picasso, Braque, Juan Gris and others.

Rivera is considered one of the greatest exponents of muralism, a more authentic pictorial movement with a profound social-artistic content that arose because of the need of the new Mexico to develop its own styles.

"Portrait of Juanita" and "Children Eating Lunch" is a living example of our people and especially of the working class. Children was one of the themes that Rivera developed with great mastery.

"Portrait of Juanita" is sitting on her feet on a "petate" (a small mat made of palm leaves) with her knees bent; her face and the position of her hands denote shyness. We can observe a reflective infantile tenderness and a national and social credo, not in terms of aggression, but one stemming from a melancholy and an unattainable beauty.

The "Children Eating Lunch" are quietly seated in front of an old stone wall, indicating to us that they are bearers of pre-Hispanic food. The boy's posture is relaxed, however that of the girl is stiff and it calls to mind indigenous figures.

DIEGO RIVERA
Portrait of Juanita
Retrato de Juanita
1935
tempera on linen /
tempera sobre lino

11

DIEGO RIVERA
Children Having Lunch
Niños almorzando
1935
oil on dry-mounting /
óleo sobre fibracel

David Alfaro Siqueiros

(Ciudad Camargo, Chihuahua, 1896-1974)

As an artist he is known by his second last name: Siqueiros which comes from his mother's side of the family. From the time he was a small child he showed tendencies towards drawing and color, and as such his parents made sure that he received classes from an academic professor. At the age of fifteen he enters the "Escuela Nacional de Bellas Artes" (National School of Fine Arts; formerly the Academy of San Carlos) in order to study arquitecture, but he is not admitted because of his age and he registers in the painting department for night classes.

In 1911 there is much political excitement in the country for Madero's revolution. At the National School of Fine Arts the students did not agree with the teaching methods, and when they held a strike Siqueiros joined them. Later he moves to Guadalajara, where he stayed until 1917, the year he returns to Mexico City. In his quest for success, he travels to Europe (Spain, France and Italy) in 1919. In Paris he meets Rivera, who was involved with the avant-garde artists of the day.

His work between 1919-21 represents his formative years, and is generally in direct contrast to the works he executed in later periods as part of his work as both a muralist and easel painter.

Siqueiros, together with Rivera and Orozco, forms the group of the "three great artists" of the muralist movement. It was supported by José Vasconcelos, Minister of Public Education, who sponsored the program to decorate public buildings with murals. The purpose of the murals was to broaden nationalism with a profound meaning, not the picturesque or superficial. Its themes were historic, political and critical.

In the work "Giving of Toys" the strokes are immense and extraordinary, and reminds one of his murals in which the artist shows an obsession for reaching the visual fields through great violence. He does this by the close-up contrasting images of the two women. The main theme is a critique of society.

DAVID ALFARO SIQUEIROS
Giving of Toys
Entrega de Juguetes
1961
oil on wood /
óleo sobre madera

José Clemente Orozco

(Zapotlán, Jalisco 1883 - Mexico City 1949)

From the age of seven he lived in Mexico City where his artistic education begins, influenced by the work of José Guadalupe Posada. He studies for four years at the Academy of San Carlos (1906-1910).

When the Mexican Revolution begins in 1910, Orozco was an active participant, allying himself with Carranza's followers. Soon he became disillusioned with the excesses of that period and he later represents them in a series of satirical drawings.

From 1917 to 1922 Orozco works in California and he returns to Mexico after government stability has been established.

He paints his first murals in the "Escuela Nacional Preparatoria" in Mexico City, in which he shows great concern for the destruction and suffering caused by the war. He also showed great concern for aesthetics in an effort to integrate form and expression.

From 1921 to 1934, he works in the United States painting murals in Pomona College, The New School for Social Research and Dartmouth College.

In 1932 he travels to Europe and visits Paris, London, Spain and Italy, where he is impressed by the medieval murals.

His most noteworthy murals are painted from 1936 to 1949 and are found in the "Museo de Bellas Artes", "Escuela Nacional de Maestros", "Conservatorio Nacional de Música", "Universidad Nacional de México", "Palacio de Gobierno" and "Hospicio Cabañas de Guadalajara".

The quality of his easel painting alone is enough to consider him a great artist. An example of this is the work "Criminals of War", whose theme is the drama of Spanish domination. His interpretation of the masacre reveals the deepest kind of historical criticism.

Orozco said: "I prefer black and the lands excluded by the impressionist's palettes. Instead of red and yellow dusk, I paint the pestilent shadows of closed rooms..."

13

JOSÉ CLEMENTE OROZCO
War Criminals
Criminales de Guerra
undated / *sin fecha*
oil on canvas / *óleo sobre tela*

33

José Chávez Morado

(Guanajuato, Guanajuato, 1909)

As a painter he considered himself self-taught: as an art activist he left an imprint on the "Liga de Escritores y Artistas Revolucionarios (The League of Revolutionary Writers and Artists LEAR), the Studio for Popular Graphic Art and the National Sculpture Front. As an engraver and sketch artist his work is of such magnitude that it would be difficult to cover all of it in a study devoted especially to his work. As a teacher he achieved the division of various disciplines while director of the School of Design and Crafts.

His obssesion is with monumental work: he does paintings in nearly twenty public and private buildings (the National University, the Medical Center, the Ministry of Communications, the "Alhóndiga de Granaditas" in Guanajuato and the Museum of Anthropology).

In " El Adobero" and "Tolteca" we note an obssesion with monumental work.

In the former he emphasizes the importance of contemporary construction. The position of the crouching laborer calls to mind the figures in the codex, the body is in almost fetal position deeply bound to the earth. In this work, he reflects an aspect of everyday life and traditions that continue to influence society today, yet which originate in the indigenous traditions of the people. The subject is surrounded by adobe walls left out to dry and he is mixing the mud into regular molds. The body acquires such proportions and the scene such a cloistered power that we could call it a homage to quiet individualism within an activity in which everythting is a game of shared attitudes.

The second work, "Tolteca" reveals a great voluminousness, like sculptured mass. Its arrangement is similar to the giant Olmec monoliths and the "Atlantes de Tula" in Hidalgo. Chávez Morado majestically captures the contrast of light and shadow. Besides, the figure is shown embracing a pyramid, multi-colored worshipping steps with their great bulky members. The material elements take on a conceptual grandeur and a sculptured strength that a few painters hav achieved by means of such apt formal materials and compositions.

JOSÉ CHÁVEZ MORADO
The Bricklayer
El Adobero
1980
oil on canvas / *óleo sobre tela*

15

JOSÉ CHÁVEZ MORADO
Tolteca
1961
oil on canvas / *óleo sobre tela*

Manuel Rodríguez Lozano

(Mexico City 1895-1971)

An independent, strange and solitary figure in our art history. In his younger years Rodríguez Lozano was closely connected with a number of artists committed to artistic nationalism: at one time he educates artists of the caliber of Julio Castellanos, Nefero or Abraham Angel; however, his introspective and profoundly critical nature lead him to adopt an intolerant and occasionally aggressive attitude towards his fellow artists, which eventually dissuades him from continuing along the artistic path. He is deeply bitter and shuts himself off from others, convincing himself that he is incapable of achieving through art the high ideals he set for himself as a young man.

"Woman Holding a Child" is a piece in which there is a noticeable lack of ability in the construction of the painting, as well as in the composition and depth of the figures. The chromatic palette is very limited and the geometric shapes that prevail in the forms are clearly seen in the outline of the figure against flat backgrounds with few contrasts. This reflects an incessant search of the painter which will end up giving strong personality to his work. Toward the end of the 1930's his figures are outlined against desolate landscapes, dissolved into flat planes, naked and isolated, intertwining themselves without any other purpose than that of the composition itself.

16

MANUEL RODRÍGUEZ LOZANO
Woman Holding a Child
Mujer con niño en brazos
1927
oil on board / *óleo sobre tabla*

Pablo O'Higgins

(Salt Lake City, Utah, United States of America, 1904 - Mexico City, 1983)

A foreign artist who wholeheartedly joins to the mural movement. In 1925 he joins the Mexican Renaissance thanks to an invitation to assist Diego Rivera in his work at the Ministry of Education and the School of Agriculture at Chapingo.

Together with Alfredo Salce and Leopoldo Mendez, he founded the Section of Plastic Arts of the League of Revolutionary Writers and Artists (LEAR).

His mural and easel work is vast. Even though he was influenced by Rivera and Orozco, he remains relatively intact, thus creating a personal style.

An example of his mural painting is that of the one made together with Leopoldo Mendez in Maternity 1 of the Mexican Institute of Health entitled "Maternity and Social Assistance," which has been totally destroyed . In the United States he painted two murals: one related with "The Struggle Against Racial Discrimination" (1945). In 1962 he finished the mural "Inside Indian Market," a tarahumara scenery and the "God of Fire," in the pre-Hispanic section of the National Museum of Anthropology.

O'Higgins´ main theme is the Mexican, who he represented in different attitudes. The painting "Ramon Gomez Varela" shows the synthesis of his aesthetic creed. An old man kneeling, tired by age and the hardship of life, his face showing melancholy in a scene full of serenity. The "sombrero charro" and "poncho," give the painter a chance to play with the brushes using extensive planes of colors with shaded strokes, allowing the viewer to presence plastic shades schematically (as the stained glass maker when he divides the areas of color...).

PABLO O'HIGGINS
Ramón Gómez Varela
1960
oil on canvas / *óleo sobre tela*

Roberto Montenegro

Guadalajara, Jalisco 1986 - Mexico, D.F. 1968)

He first studies art in his hometown under the instruction of provincial teachers. His relative, the poet Amado Nervo, helped him to go to Mexico City where he entered the National School of Fine Arts in order to register in the school of architecture. Unable to achieve this purpose, he went into painting, where he soon excelled in drawing. His classmates were Saturnino Herrán, Diego Rivera and José Clemente Orozco.

In Montenegro there was an admirable aptitude for decoration, drawing and color. In 1906, he competed with Rivera for a fellowship in Madrid and won, ennrolling into the academy of San Fernando. While in Europe, the First World War erupted and he lived four years in confinement on the island of Mallorca. In 1920, he returned to Mexico and began his decorative art, entering the mural school.

In his work "Child with Parrot", one can observe Diego Rivera's influence and although he is somewhat careless, he had a talent for drawing and a sense of color. The subject is a brown child with a scarf around his head in denim overalls, painted in a rather slack form and with some laziness.

"The Green Apple" is a confused composition. The abuse of black is broken by a minimum of cold shades, bittersweet, which gives the scene an unreal hue that runs throughout

The shaping of "motionless things" in this composition is congruent with the title of "still life," but it is categorized into that of inactive objects, since the artist blends rocks, stone fruits carved in marble and onyx, fragments of a disarticulated doll, a polycrystal, a small case with a hard rock such as malachite, into a whole, wrapped and surrounded with rock formations

The subject is presented at the beginning in shades of whites, greens and yellows, and later twisted by contrasting blacks.

18

ROBERTO MONTENEGRO
Child with Parrot
Niño con periquito
undated / *sin fecha*
oil on canvas / *óleo sobre tela*

ROBERTO MONTENEGRO
The Green Apple
La manzana verde
1964
oil on masonite / *óleo sobre mansonite*

Federico Cantú

Cadereyta de Jimenez, N.L., 1908 - Mexico D. F., 1989)

The great Mexican historian, Justino Fernández, said that in his paintings one could see a passionate temperament, full of contrasts; a practical world, pagan and religious at the same time.

The main subject in his paintings was the religious, represented by angels, sacred families, and passages of Christ's life. Among them, we can mention "God the Father" and "Cana's Wedding." There is a mural made by him at the viceroyalty's art gallery with a religious theme, portraying the conversion of the indigenous culture by the Franciscan monks.

In the painting "Cana's Wedding," Christ appears in the center, blessing the wine gourd of abundance, camouflaging himself among the people at the marketplace, not congregating at a wedding banquet; the third area or first level is disconnected from the main theme. The artist has the obsession to use the repetition of strokes, thus loosing the level's distance and the sensation of distance.

The Biblical scenes take place among the Indians and the grouping of characters give the impression of a popular painter. It is here where Cantu tries to revive a strong and well-rooted tradition in the history of our paintings, which, at the same time, represents one of the most beautiful of its facets.

46

20

FEDERICO CANTÚ
God the Father
Dios Padre
1965
oil on canvas / *óleo sobre tela*

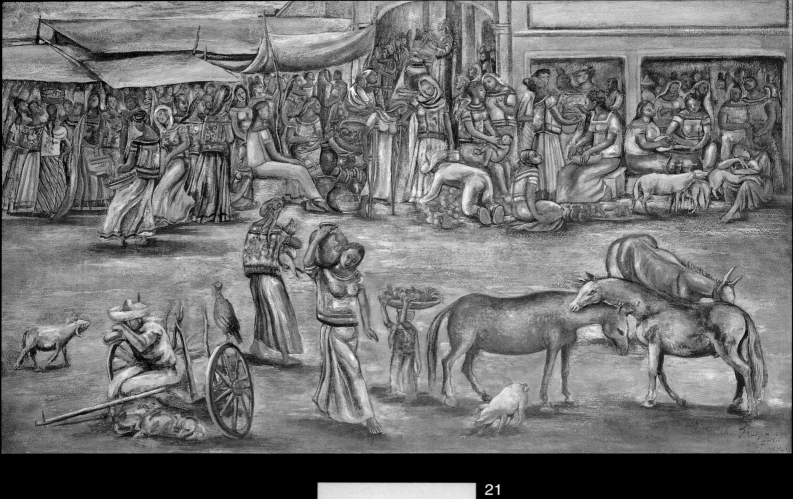

21

FEDERICO CANTÚ
Cana's Wedding
Las Bodas de Caná
1951
oil on canvas / *óleo sobre tela*

Emilio Baz y Viaud

(1918-?)

There is very little background about this painter. It is known
that he was born in 1918 and that as a youngster he began his
studies in architecture, soon finding his vocation to painting. He
took courses at the National School of Plastic Arts and met
Manuel Rodriguez Lozano, who taught him the basis of a strict
discipline. His works are influenced by Julio Castellanos,
Roberto Montenegro and Diego Rivera.

After spending some time in New York, he resided in San Miguel
Allende, until he joined the Benedictine order in 1950.
 His favourite subjects are portraits, folklore scenes and the great
compositions. Through these works he always obtained
equilibrium and great colour.

In his work "Mexican Indian" a big, strong, sensual, compact,
bulky, image appears. I could even call it a sculpturesque face,
covering the whole composition. Despite its aggressive
dimensions, the look reflects a certain melancholy and delicacy in
the strokes. The painting brings us close to other faces of our
plastic paintings, as those of Diego Rivera, Montenegro and Best
Maugard, who also created huge faces covering the entire work.

22

EMILIO BAZ Y VIAUD
Mexican Indian
India mexicana
1939
gouache and watercolor /
gouache y acuarela cartón

Miguel Covarrubias

Mexico City, 1904 - 1957)

He appears in the world of painting at the age of eighteen. In 1920, he leaves the Preparatory school and rejects any academic education; he publishes his first caricatures in student and literary magazines. He works as a cartoonist for the Communications Secretariat and becomes friends with Rivera, Siqueiros, Orozco, Montenegro, etc.
A year later, he made caricatures for the "Heraldo" and "Universal" newspapers.

In 1923, he goes to New York, where he achieves fame as a cartoonist, and becomes the official cartoonist of the magazine Vanity Fair, until 1936.
  In 1930, he marries Rosa Rolanda in Kentcliffe, New York, after which he remained in Bali for nine months.

Ten years later, he paints two murals for the World´s Fair in San Francisco of the economic map of America. Using the same style, but related to Mexico, he created the two panels exhibited at the "Hotel del Prado," which were destroyed by the earthquake of 1985.

Covarrubias gives classes of pre-Hispanic and primitive art at the National School of Anthropology in 1943, and three years later, he is appointed Chief of the Dancing Department of the National Institute of Fine Arts.

The painting "Balinesa" is repeated in most of his works. The idyllic beauty with slim, earthen colored torso, brilliant eyes and splendid red lips was a re-occurent theme. The colors have the spontaneity and the dazzling freshness of the jungle.
 His overlaping strokes are small, giving the surface a velvet-like or soft texture, with inner sparks and unexpected contrasts.

23

MIGUEL COVARRUBIAS
Balinesa
undated / *sin fecha*
oil on canvas / *óleo sobre tela*

Raul Anguiano

Guadalajara, Jalisco 1915)

Together with other artists he organized the group "Young Painters of Jalisco," in his home town. At the age of 19, he went to Mexico City where he is later appointed Secretary General of the Union of Plastic Arts' Teachers.

Throughout his works, he had maintained a faithful realistic tendency, which he enriches with fantastic elements.

Anguiano develops prints, drawings, paintings, and murals (National Museum of Anthropology) dealing with the essential themes of the Mexican Revolution. Besides his vocation for painting, he studied ethnology, a subject which he loves and further develops mainly about the women of the Lacandona area.

The young "Yalalteca," masterly braided with dark ribbons, abandons herself in inertia, displaying a serene beauty in her face, with bare extremities. Anguiano uses the contrast of lights and shadows to enhance her musculature.

With great expertise the painter uses the human figure to show abandonment, fragility, and transitory beauty, as well as the haughtiness of her face and the magnificence of her body through the brushstrokes of color, applied one by one.

24

RAÚL ANGUIANO
Yalalteca
1977
oil on canvas / *óleo sobre tela*

Two experiences took place during Maria's childhood that left marks and later shaped the subjects of her paintings: one, is an accident occurred when she was the victim of a horse stampede in which she was not injured but that left deep emotional scars; the other, was her escapade at the age of two with a travelling circus.

In 1928, she enrolls in the Academy of Painting and Sculpture of the Ministry of Education where she stays only a year due to the monotonous routine and conservatism. She received her first stimulus from Diego Rivera and Rufino Tamayo. Fernando Gamboa assures that "Tamayo tought her everything, from watercolor... (he) educates her taste and trains her eye..." On the other hand, Inés Amor stipulates the influence María had on Tamayo saying that it is she who teaches the "Maestro" a languaje and a different style of painting. "María painted with her indian blood on the tip of her brush. Thus, Tamayo emerged, surpassing all other colleagues".

María Izquierdo's work distinguishes itself in that it is a free and spontaneous expression with outstandingly strong contrasts.

"Girls with Watermelon" is a painting in which realism is superimposed on that which seems unreal; the landscape of reddish trees is lined up as a succesion of brittle corpses; this interspacial relation of forms reminds us of abandoned train stations, always in ruins, disarray and desolation.

Both girls, looking at the inviting fruit, evoke a formal language, whose expressiveness, freshness and enchantment are the product of certain inconsistencies of techniques as well as the rigidity of artists such as José María Estrada and Hermemegildo Bustos. These XXc painters departed from the formal Academy guidelines, structuring a unique, formal language.

The painting "Girl with Red Hat" shows a marked tendency toward the massive found in Olmec sculpture. The "Mexicanicity" of its protagonists is accented by native features full of tenderness.

In the painting of backdrops used by village photographers, María interprets them using highly resolved grissaille through which swans, clouds, vases and columns appear. In other words, there are various ill-matched colors giving the composition great chromatic vibrancy and a sense of its own volume.

María Izquierdo

(San Juan de los Lagos,1902- Mexico City, 1955)

As a child, she is her grandparent's caretaker. After her father's death she travels to Torreón with her mother. Her childhood is rooted in the customs and rituals of rural life whose rich Mexican traditions she treasures for the rest of her life.

25

MARÍA IZQUIERDO
Girls with Watermelon
Niñas con sandía
1946
oil on canvas / *óleo sobre tela*

26

MARÍA IZQUIERDO
Girl with Red Hat
Niña con sombrero rojo
1942
oil on canvas / *óleo sobre tela*

Frida Kahlo

Mexico, D.F., 1910-1954)

A painter always accepted into the Mexican artistic circle even though her works were a notable divergence from the forms which were characteristic of the Mexican school. The daughter of a well-known photographer, a German immigrant, Guillermo Kahlo gave her the capacity to perceive Mexican reality.

As a child she was affected by polio, and in 1925 (at the age of 19) she was the victim of a serious bus accident, which modified her personality and life, leaving severe wounds and intermittent periods of paralysis. She underwent several surgeries, ending in the amputation of a leg. She began to paint after the accident and developed her art almost in an autodidactic way. In 1929 she married Diego Rivera and they became the central couple in the artistic and intellectual Mexican society.

In 1937 she met Breton (the beginner of the surrealist theory) in Paris and began to get in touch with the surrealists.

Breton postulated that Frida Kahlo's art was like "a ribbon around a bomb".
In her painting "Portrait of Isolda Pinedo Kahlo," there were not yet those fantastic elements which qualified her as a surrealistic painter, since it was made before she entered that movement. The work is reduced to purely academic; her love for the popular is reflected in the rag doll, abandoned and reclining, which is being disincorporated from the infant figure.

The work "My Dress Hangs Here," was painted by Kahlo while she was living in the United States, forming in it a complex symbolism, but making clear her aesthetic preference for Mexican art, by the Tehuana dress hanging from a rope.

In the lower part of the painting, she introduced the technique of "collage," having several independent groups which, at a glance, give the impression of being painted in great detail, showing a preoccupation for delicate work and achieving surprising qualities.

27

FRIDA KAHLO
Portrait of Isolda Pinedo Kahlo
Retrato de Isolda Pinedo Kahlo
1929
oil on canvas / *óleo sobre tela*

28

FRIDA KAHLO
My Dress hangs here
Mi vestido cuelga aquí
1933
oil and collage masonite /
óleo y collage masonite

Gunther Gerzo

(Mexico City, 1915)

After acquiring an extensive cultural background in Europe, he studies scenography in Cleveland, Ohio dedicating the following years to designing scenery for the national film industry.

The free spirited Gerzo always kept up with the different trends in contemporary art.

Influenced by Leonora Carrington, Remedios Varo, the poet Benjamín Peret, Alico Rahon and Wolfgong Paalen (surrealists), he delves into surrealistic painting even though his output is quite limited. He later radically modifies his style entering a period of tranquility, order and self-discipline. His repertoire is in most part of his paintings defined by geometric structures, almost always asymetric, reaching levels of abstraction through mathematic compositions using color as the primary point of departure.

His painting "Blue Planes" enters abstract geometrics. Abstract art is when the spectator, while observing cannot translate precise images (it neither tells a story or reflects the world around us) On many occasions the qualitative goes against the artist's best intentions. Gerzo himself said " *Why do they define me as an abstract painter?....if we already know that all art is abstract".*

"Yes, (replied Teresa del Conde), but you, since the paintings you produced after your first trip to Greece, ignored elements that directly remind us of objects and images". His reaction to this remark surprised her: "But I am a landscape artist...! My paintings are of the ruins of Labná, of the Lacandon jungle or of everything I can now see from this window".

GUNTHER GERZSO
Blue Planes
Planos en Azul
1965
oil on dry-mounting /
óleo sobre fibracel

Rafael Coronel

Zacatecas, Zacatecas, 1932).

At the beginning Rafael leaned towards architecture, but gradually changed to painting, and began to study in the so called "Taller libre," directed by Carlos Orozco Romero at the National School of Fine Arts.

His first works were based on the permanent search for the essential visual values in painting, such as texture, composition, color, form, and tactile material, thus creating the appearance of his favourite subjects, masks, planimetric movements originated by animals, etc.

Together with his brother Pedro, they collected heterogeneous objects, placing them among the most important art collectors in our country.

"Christ" is one of the best synthesis of the moral pain of Mexicans. His skin becomes a porous surface in which the greys, the gathering shadows, the cropping out of the white face and the shades of red, offer to the viewer a diverse gamut of pasty shades, bringing out the fading of time. The work leans towards an expressionism, as far as the rejection of beauty as end all to achieve the conventional . Its world is being expressed in shades, as passion causes an excessive tension against forms, violence accentuate contrasts, petrified energy gives life to figure.

"The Herb Vendor" and "Child with Baby Doll" eminate dramatism and beauty as perceived by the impressionists. There is no perfection in forms, the ideal proportion or the strict symmetry; but it is in the character, force, energy, and deep expression where Coronel knew how to bound literary and formal baroque as expressionist beauty.

RAFAEL CORONEL
Christ
Cristo
1956
oil on canvas / *óleo sobre tela*

31

RAFAEL CORONEL
The Herb Vendor
El Yerbero
1973
oil on canvas / *óleo sobre tela*

RAFAEL CORONEL
Child with Baby Doll
Niño con Muñeca
undated / *sin fecha*
oil on canvas / *óleo sobre tela*

Pedro Coronel

(Zacatecas, 1922-1985)

He studies at the National School of Painting and Sculpture of Mexico City developing a great interest for captivating, interpreting and transmiting the prehispanic heritage and also for submiting his art to the occidental schools of art.

He is part of a generation which, stimulated by Rufino Tamayo, explores the figure of color, the presence of myths and new relations between figure and space.

"Celestial Navigators", full of traces, textures and chromatic counterpoints, places the sun at the center of his composition, without luminosity, identified by shadows.

The oil he applies through heavy coats leaves it crackeled like the bark of trees.

The work "Head" demonstrates his preference for the indigenous world, with the magnificent mythical and religious creations produced before the conquest. This piece shows the violent contrast of pure and direct colors enriched with rich harmonies and textures as the ones used in "Fantasy Corners II".

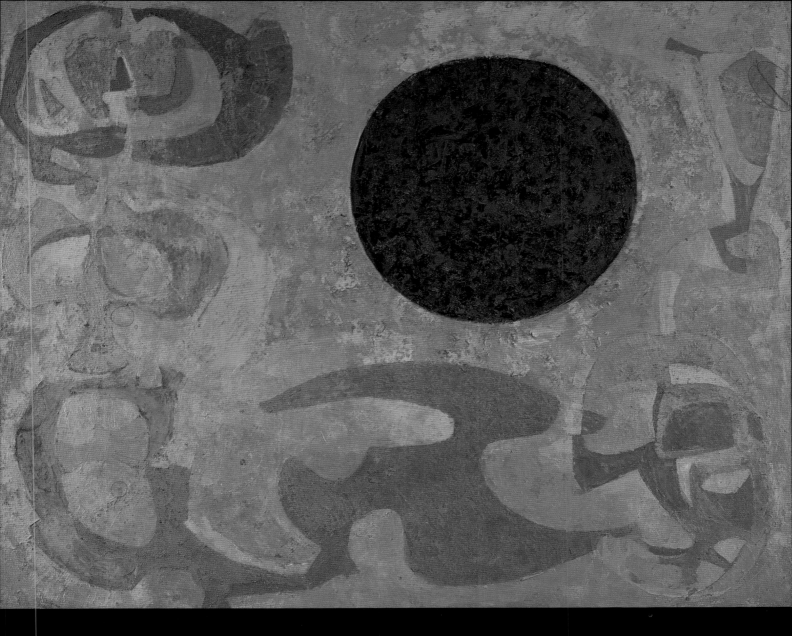

33

PEDRO CORONEL
Celestial Navigators
Navegantes celestes
undated / *sin fecha*
oil on canvas / *óleo sobre tela*

34

PEDRO CORONEL
Head
Cabeza
undated / *sin fecha*
oil on canvas / *óleo sobre tela*

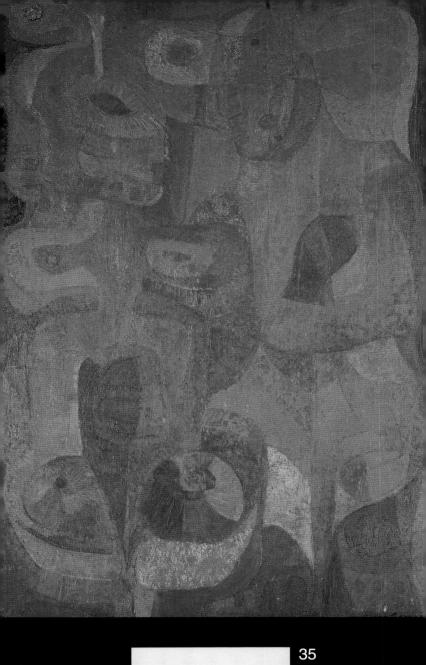

35

PEDRO CORONEL
Fantasy Corners II
Rincones de ensueño II
undated / *sin fecha*
oil on canvas / *óleo sobre tela*

Francisco Corzas

(Mexico City, 1933)

His childhood is spent in the bosom of a family of laborers with an uncle who, as toymaker and tatoo artist, most likely influenced on him at the beginning of his artistic career. This uncle used empty cans to make toys, butterflies and as Corzas himself said: *"He also painted lovely faces, like those found in the school of Art Nouveau. We were dealing with an urban wanderer, a madman...."*. It was the uncle himself who taught him about the harsh reality of the needy, and Corzas, used violence to protect himself against its pain.

His talents as an artist could be detected even as a child as he painted recurrent themes of open winged butterflies and Christs in pencil on the bathroom walls. At 14, and thanks to a teacher that helps him in waiving fees, he enrolls in the Esmeralda School of Painting and Sculpture to take some painting courses.

Corzas is always against the established canons of the Academy. His form of expression is very different from the norm of those times.

From 1956 to 59, he travels to Europe, living in Rome where he takes courses in fresco painting at the Academy of San Giacomo and nudes at the Fine Arts. His main themes are those of the homeless, of couples, nudes, mystical animals and extravaganzas.

He admires the art of the old maestros such as: Velázquez, Rembrandt, Caravaggio and Goya, among others.

In "Portrait of Sandra", Corzas draws a woman with a blind stare, lost in the infinite, absorbed in a void. She eminates an agonizing serenity and communicates a sense of mellodeous beauty. The figure looks capriciously dressed in an out of season attire, in other words, not in sync with the times.

Corzas paints the woman as something enigmatic: *"My subjects are aparitions, being that are found anywhere...".*

He uses mostly earth-colours, adding a little luminous tone.

To describe Corzas and to attempt to decipher his meaning is no easy task. What can be said is that his painting has a close similarity with that from Spain and that it is first and foremeost, a long, profound meditation and metaphor of the shattering human condition.

36

FRANCISCO CORZAS
Portrait of Sandra
Retrato de Sandra
1978
oil on canvas / *óleo sobre tela*

Olga Dondé

(Campeche, 1937)

She presents several individual exhibits in Washington, D.C., Texas, Bogotá and Caracas. Among the collective exhibitions in which she participates is the Solar Exhibit at the Palace of Fine Arts in Mexico and at the Museum of Contemporary Art of Bogotá.

Dondé also makes scenery and costumes for theatre plays.

In her painting "Quality of life:Fig" there is a great chromatic contrast. The texture gives the fruit enourmous realism, inviting the public to taste it.

Olga Dondé associates her search with the offering of flavours, the gastronomic pleasure and the texture contact, obtaining the goal which the XVII Century painters of Flanders and the Netherlands sought in their still lives: the simultaneous association of the senses and the appetite they tend to provoke.

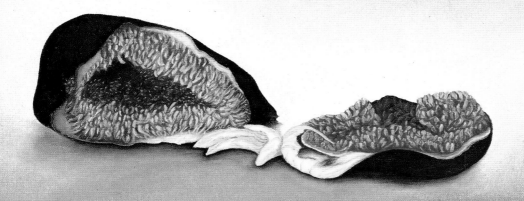

Dondé
méjico septiembre 1º 1974

37

OLGA DONDÉ
Quality of Life: Fig
Calidad de vida, higo
1974
oil on canvas / *óleo sobre tela*

Jesús Reyes Ferreira

(Guadalajara, Jal. 1882- México D.F.,1977)

When he was 14 years old, he starts as an apprentice at Loreto Anoira's lithographic workshop. In 1938 he moves to Mexico City dedicating most of his time to painting.

Ferreira, an expert in Mexican art, was consulted by collectors, critics and artists.

Architect Luis Barragán introduces him to a wide group of architects. Their appreciation of Mexican art opened new horizons in design, architecture and urbanism.

He travels to Europe and the East in 1972: he exhibits his works in Barcelona and produces graphic works; he continues making experiments in the artistic field.

The "Christ in Three Parts" has an unsual dimension compared with his other artworks, containing peculiar spots spread in order to cover the white spaces.

In most of his Christian iconographic works, Reyes continues the popular beliefs in a simple and accidental way, accenting the lack of resources: the ingenuity of his line, the scarcity of instruments and the absence of technique.

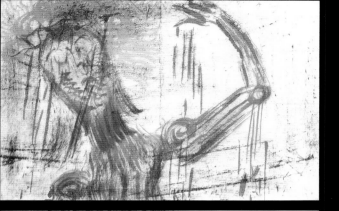

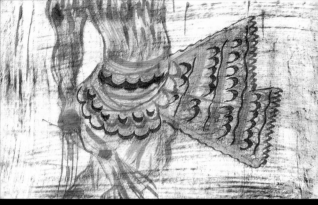

38

JESÚS REYES FERREIRA
Christ in Three Parts
Cristo en tres partes
undated / *sin fecha*
gouache on paper /
gouache sobre papel

contemporary
art

To speak of Mexican folkart is to allude to social art, to that instance in which man is given a sense of belonging to a place and a group. It is to refer to a well known art inasmuch as it channels a specific vision of the world, yet is a result of a collective will, of a traditional dynamic meeting its need to recreate, to transfigure the world, to become artistically sensitive.

eing at one with the materialization of culture, folkart is present in the many spheres of the Mexican social life. Popular artists inject life into inanimate materials creating objects that accompany the Mexican in the most dis-symbolic experiences of his life: they go with him to the dining table and to the "fiestas", they take on life through native costumes and dances, they appear when evoking the dead and relating to the living, they are never absent from religious ceremonies.

Folkart acquires cultural significance only when contextualized, when it is reffered to and inserted into the cultures that have produced it. Behind folkart the relations established between society-man-nature become interactive with the materials that mold them. The same thing occurs with the technological processes created by man and the material and spiritual requirements needed for such objects....

But if Mexican folkart is correctly conceptualized, it is possible not only to grasp the interaction of elements but also to read the cosmovision of the group members. They are fleetingly expressed and re-created in a myriad of forms shaped into tangible objects, full of symbolisms related to the cultural expressions, without which they would lose meaning.

In addition to the interaction and concept of the universe contained within the expression of folkart, we find the synthesis of the aspects which define our culture. No other artistic expression renders faithful testimony of the elements used in their creation. It is a mirror image of our history, of the sensitivity, creativity and imagination of our people.

Like our culture, folkart is constantly changing. It creates a dynamic which opposes the stagnation in the struggle and evolution of its social-historic moment. This phenomena, this transformation projects onto the techniques and designs, onto the innovations, even onto the shapes which eventually distort its cultural or artistic integrity.

Mexico is, therefore, a mosaic of cultures, a mixture of groups and races. The native's beliefs, uses, customs and ideals of earthly life and life beyond combined without dissipation or loss - with the cosmovision of Europe and Africa.

The Spaniards, who were the inheritors of the Arab and African cultures, made contributions that neither abolished or invalidated the originals. They promoted the appearance of new cultural initiatives departing from their own patterns while preserving the identity of the country. A similar process took place with the arrival of a vast and heterogenic gamut of ethnic groups to Mexico: English, French, Italian, German, Chinese, Middle East colonies and later on, American, giving way to cultural pluralism and the diversity which so distinguishes Mexico.

Today, each region, group and class that shapes Mexican society has its individual culture. Naturally, common traces and elements exist such as land, language, law, economics, national symbols, etc. In fact, the ethnic cultures and popular stratus incorporate common traces into their regional style, adopt them, but do not necessarily lose their individuality.

Therefore, culture's affiliation with the nation identifies basically with its origin, its inspiration, its source of development. As Diego Rivera said: "the more native the art, the more it belongs to the world", indicating that the more national the expression of culture, the closer they are to the people's experience, the more universal they become.....One must not lose sight of the fact that behind this complex process of social group formation one finds cultural creativity, the capacity of making individual initiatives to identify and solve problems, and that these cultural initiatives are not born in a vaccum: they rely on the acquisition of experience and knowledge from the cultural repertoire of various groups. For this very reason there is change and continuity in the transformation of cultures. For this reason folkart expresses the initiatives, the dynamic of a feeling, keeping rythm with the human circumstance, with the transformation of oneself.

That is why Mexican folkart ranks among the best. It has the capacity to materialize and channel the diversity of elements in popular cultures shaping the magnificent art of the nation.

Ma. Esther Echeverría Zuno, Anthropologist

39

**JOSÉ ELOY
RODRÍGUEZ VALENCIA**
Blue Bridle with Silver Inlay
Freno azul con incrustación de plata
silver / *plata pavonada*
Amozoc de Mota, Pue.

40

SIMÓN CONTRERAS CAPILLA
Hand Basin
Platón Palangana
Talavera
San Pablo del Monte, Tlax.

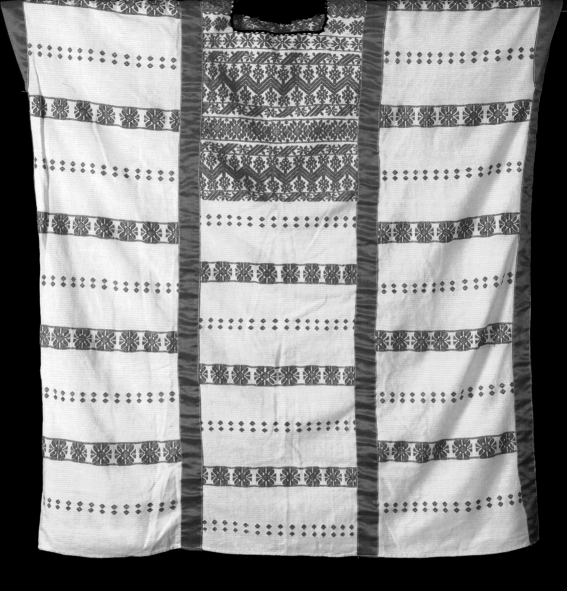

**TOMASA HERNÁNDEZ
MARTÍNEZ**
Red Huipil
Huipil rojo
waist weaving loom /
tejido en telar de cintura
cotton textile / *textil en algodón*
San Pedro Amuzgos, Oax.

**ROGELIO HERNÁNDEZ
ANTONIO**
■─────────────■
Reed Water Car
Carro pipa de carrizo natural
sliced reed grass /
carrizo cortado y ensamblado
San Juan Guelavia, Oax.

43

JOSÉ GARCÍA BAUTISTA
Bookcase
Librero cómoda
Engraved Zirimo Wood
Madera de Zirimo ensamblada
y grabada.
Guanajuato, Mich.

MANUEL VALENCIA CHÁVEZ
Mask and Cap for the Black Dance / *Máscara y gorra para danza de los negros*
polychromated carved wood / *madera tallada policromada*
Sevina, Mich.

44

87

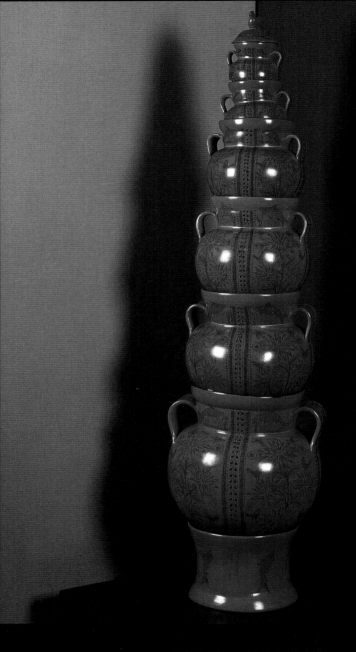

ELENA FELIPE FÉLIX
6 Pot Tower (Flowers and Birds)
Torre de 6 ollas (motivo flores y aves)
moulded and brunished clay /
barro modelado y bruñido
Huancito, Mich.

46

**BERNARDO MÁRQUEZ Y
MADRIGAL**
Vendor Couple
Pareja de vendedores
Panicua tejida
knited hard and soft fibers
fibras duras y semi duras tejidas
San Jerónimo, Purinchécuaro, Mich.

OSCAR GRANIZO TOVAR
Little Black Dance Horse
Caballito de danza negro
carved wood / *madera tallada*
Villas de San José, Cd. del Maíz,
S.L.P.

48

LORENZO NARANJO E.
Wooden Indian Monkey
Mono indio de madera
polychromated and carved wood /
madera tallada y policromada
Ejido San José, Cd. del Maíz,
S.L.P.

49

CIPRIANO PÉREZ
Wooden Indian
Indio de Madera
polychromated and carved wood /
madera tallada y policromada
Ejido San José, Cd. del Maíz,
S.L.P.

50

MANUEL PÉREZ
Gorilla with Snake
Gorila con víbora
polychromated and carved wood /
madera tallada y policromada
Ejido San José, Cd. del Maíz,
S.L.P.

91

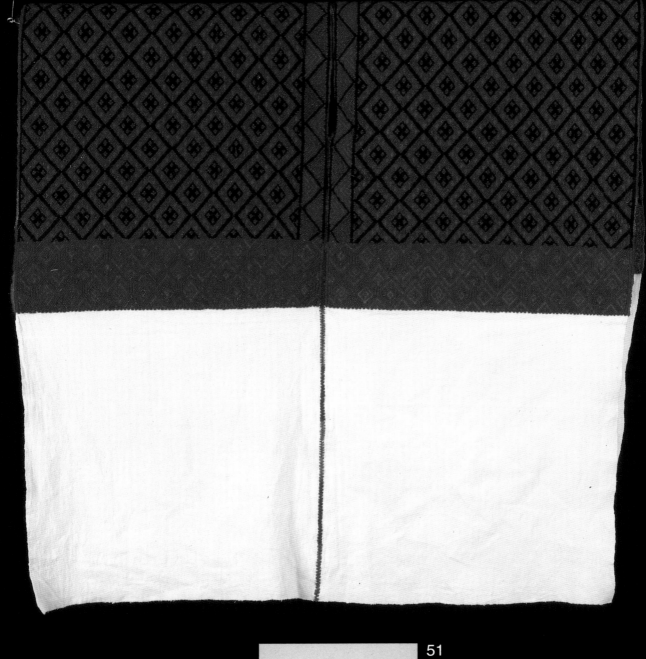

51

SEBASTIÁN GÓMEZ PÉREZ
Ceremonial Huipil
Huipil Ceremonial
waist weaving loom wool textile /
textil en lana tejido en telar
de cintura
Chacoma, Chiapas

52

ASUNCIÓN COBOS CRUZ
Three Musical Instrument Set
Juego de tres instrumentos musicales
assembled wood /
madera ensamblada
México, D.F.

53

JOSÉ ENRIQUE GALICIA FUENTES
Thirty Musical Instrument Set
Juego de treinta instrumentos musicales
jointed wood /
madera ensamblada
Mexico, D.F.

54

ALFONSO CASTILLO ORTA
Mexico's Wealth (Tree of Life)
La riqueza de México (árbol de la vida)
moulded clay polychromated with
natural tints / *barro moldeado*
policromado con tintes naturales
Izucar de Matamoros, Pue.

55

REGINA REYNOSO THIELEN
The Mourning Virgen
La Virgen de Dolores
decorated glass / *vidrio decorado*
México, D.F.

RAÚL DE JESÚS ESPINOSA VÁZQUEZ
Fish
Peces
cedar carved wood /
madera de cedro tallada
Papantla, Ver.

57

**GILBERTO GONZÁLEZ
CÓRDOVA**
Top and "Valero" (Mexican Toy)
Trompo y valero
turned walnut tree wood /
madera de nogal torneada
México, D.F.

58

**FRANCISCO CORONEL
NAVARRO**
Large Sewing Box
Costurero grande
decorated lacquer with gold 23.5 K. /
laca decorada con oro de 23.5 K.
Olinalá, Gro.

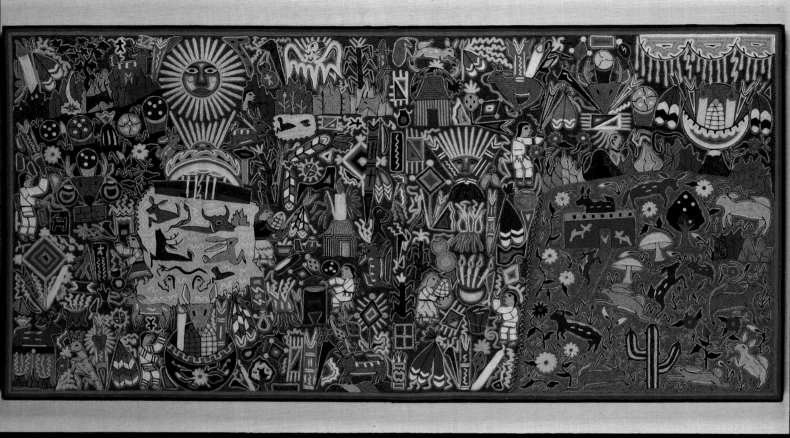

CELESTINO REZA MIJAREZ
Fiesta (Tabla Huichola)
yarn pressed on Campeche wax /
*estambre pegado con cera de
Campeche*
San Andrés Cohamiata, Jal.

INOCENCIA GONZÁLEZ
Willow Bark Skirt
Falda de corteza de sauce
knitted fibers (waist) /
tejido de fibras (cintura)
Comunidad Cucapa, B.C.

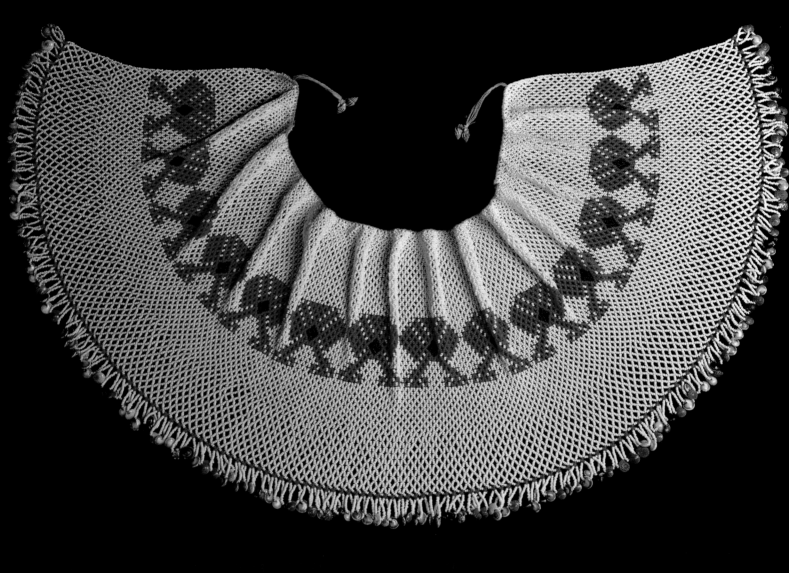

61

INOCENCIA GONZÁLEZ
Pectoral
beaded macrame /
macramé con chaquira
Comunidad Cucapa, B.C.

62

FLORENTINA LÓPEZ DE JESÚS

Brocaded Huipil
Huipil Brocado
waist loom brocade (textile cotton)
/ brocado en telar de cintura (textil algodón)
Xochistlahuaca, Gro.

63

SOFÍA FERRER GONZÁLEZ
Mazahua Doll
Muñeca mazahua
stuffed cloth /
trapo recortado y relleno
San Felipe Santiago, Edo. de Mex.

64

EFRAÍN ROMERO SALINAS
Jorongo
pedal weaving loom /
tejido en telar de pedal
Xonacatlán, Edo. de Mex.

65

PEDRO CELESTINO CELIS
The Nine Angels' Respect and Promise
*El respeto y la promesa de los
nueve angeles*
brush drawing on bark / *dibujo a
pincel en papel amate*
Xalitla, Gro.

MAGDIEL GARCÍA HERNÁNDEZ

Decorated Bottle with Mexican Eagles

Botella decorada con águilas mexicanas

engraved glass /
vidrio grabado con punta
México, D.F.

67

JOSÉ LUIS GRANIZO TOVAR
King Mask
Máscara Rey
carved wood / *madera tallada*
Villas de San José, Cd. del Maíz,
S.L.P.

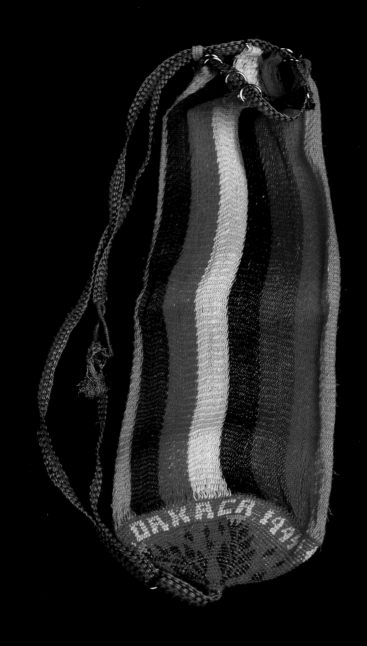

68

**FORTUNATO HERNÁNDEZ
BAZÁN**
Colored Agave Net
Red de pita de colores
knitted agave hard and soft fibers
/ *pita tejida en macramé (fibras
duras y semiduras)*
San Pedro Cajonos, Oax.

69

IRMA CANSECO MORGAN
Pitcher Lamp
Cántaro lámpara
black moulded and latticed clay /
barro negro modelado y calado
San Bartolo Coyotepec, Oax.

70

IRMA GARCÍA REYES
Seven Leaf Set
Juego de siete hojas
tissue paper cutout /
papel de china picado
Papantla, Ver.

1

BENITA MARTÍNEZ RUIZ
Doll Bell
Campana muñeca
moulded decorated clay / *barro*
modelado y decorado al pastillaje
San Miguel Aguascalientes, Ver.

**ADOLFO Y ABEL
DOMÍNGUEZ SÁINZ**
Eagle Devouring a Snake
Aguila devorando una serpiente
carved wood / *madera de
calabozo tallada*
Alto Lucero, Ver.

72

113

LA TRINIDAD
Undulated Fruit Dish
Frutero de ondas
majolica and talavera /
mayólica y talavera
Puebla, Pue.

**OLIVER VELÁZQUEZ
SERRANO**
Hispanic Native Drum
Tambor autóctono hispánico
carved wood / *madera tallada*
Suchiapa, Chis.

REINA DE MEXICO

EMPERATRIZ DE AMERICA
SANTA MARIA DE GUADALUPE
RUEGA SEÑORA POR NOSOTROS.
"ERES LA LUZ EN LAS TINIEBLAS DE LA VIDA"

LEYDI J.B.

75

LEYDI JIMÉNEZ BOJORQUEZ
Virgin of Guadalupe's Guild Banner
*Estandarte de Gremio Virgen de
Guadalupe*
embroidery / *bordado con hilo iris*
Mani, Yuc.

El Santo Patrono de Iztapalapa

76

LEONEL SALAZAR MARRUJO
The Patron Saint of Iztapalapa
El Santo Patrono de Iztapalapa
papier maché / *papel maché*
México, D.F.

77

TITO RUTILO CIPRIANO
Daily Life
La vida diaria
painted papier maché /
papel maché pintado
Xalitla, Gro.

118

78

FRUCTUOSO ZALAPA LUNA
Seventh Guitar
Guitarra séptima
assembled wood /
madera ensamblada
México, D.F.

119

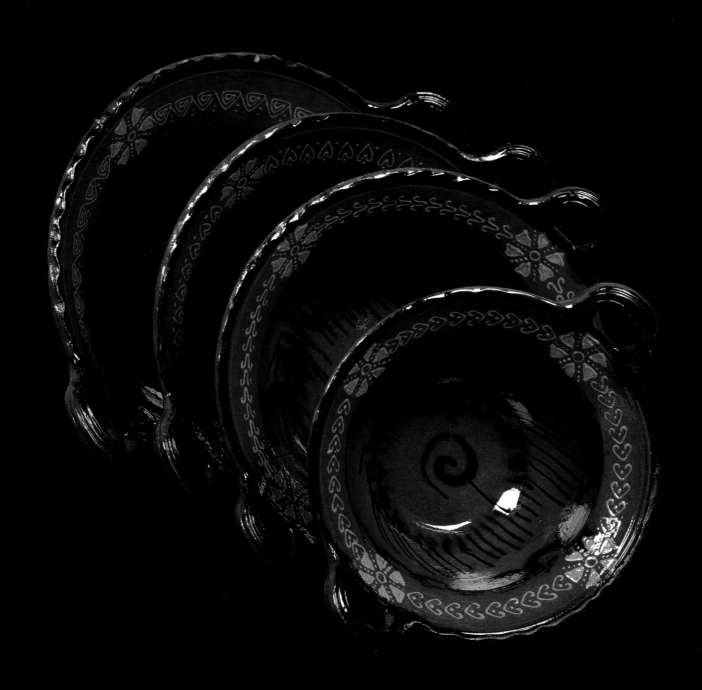

INOCENTE CASTILLO DEL AGUILA

Four Cazuela Set
Juego de cuatro cazuelas
moulded clay / *barro moldeado*
Metepec, Edo. de Mex.

80

JERÓNIMO LÓPEZ MÉNDEZ
Bullskin Mask
Máscara de piel de toro
folded and sewed bullskin /
piel de toro doblada y cosida
Col. San Marcos, Ocosingo, Chis.

81

**ARTURO ESTRADA
Y CIRILA GONZÁLEZ**
Silk Reboso
Reboso de seda
waist loom / *telar de cintura*
Santa María del Río, S.L.P.

82

FRANCISCA POSAR QUIRÓZ
Skeleton Horse
Caballo esqueleto
moulded, polychromated and
lacquered clay / *barro modelado,*
policromado y laqueado
Ocumicho, Mich.

83

JOSÉ LUIS CERDA BÁEZ
Three Piece Dish and Bowl
Cupboard
Trastero tinajero de 3 piezas
carved wood / *madera tallada*
Pátzcuaro, Mich.

84

JUSTA MATEO CRUZ
Pichancha
moulded and latticed clay /
barro modelado y calado
San Marcos Tlapazola, Oax.

85

HIPÓLITO LÓPEZ ORTEGA
Farriswheel
Rueda de la Fortuna
carved and painted wood /
madera tallada y pintada
San Martín Tilcajete, Oax.

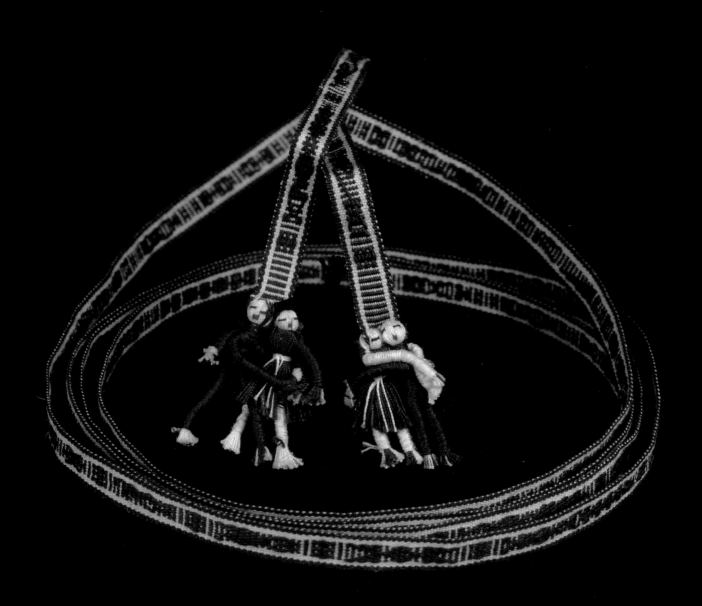

GLORIA MENDOZA LUIS
Fine Girdle
Faja fina
waist weaving loom /
tejido en telar de cintura
Santo Tomás Jalietza, Oax.

87

ISAÍ VERA CARRILLO
Tray
Bandeja
moulded and polished clay /
barro modelado y bruñido
Los Reyes Metzontla, Pue.

88

MARÍA CARMEN PULIDO
Jewelry Box
Alhajero
carved wood / *madera tallada*
Apaseo el Alto, Gto.

89

PEDRO JIMÉNEZ ANZUETO
Tenderness
(Lacandon boy with spider monkey)
Ternura
(niño lacandón con mono araña)
one piece carved wood /
madera tallada a una sola pieza
Chiapa de Corzo, Chis.

130

90

MARÍA ANTONIA PÉREZ HERNÁNDEZ
Camarín
lacquer decorated with oil
laca fondeada y decorada al óleo
Chiapa de Corzo, Chis.

91

OLMEC CENTER
CENTRO OLMECA
fine silver .925 / *plata fina .925*

92

GUAJE OLINALÁ
fine silver .925 / *plata fina .925*

133

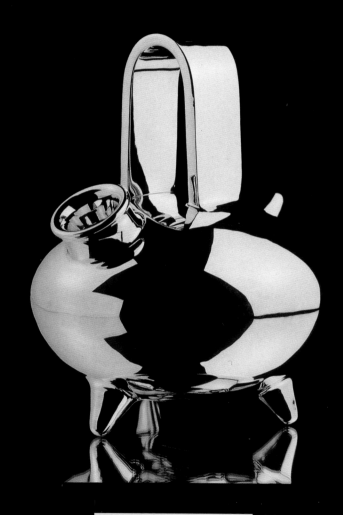

93

JALISCO JAR
JARRA JALISCO
fine silver .925 / *plata fina .925*

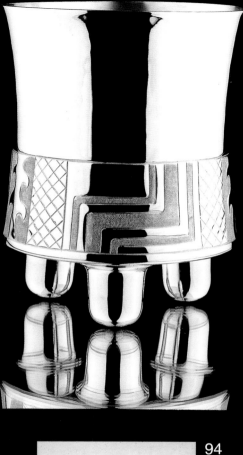

TRIPOD VESSEL FROM XOLALPAN CHICO'S
VASIJA TRÍPODE DE XOLALPAN CHICO
fine silver .925 / *plata fina .925*

95

MAYAN TRIPOD BOWL
CAJETE TRÍPODE MAYA
fine silver .925 / *plata fina .925*

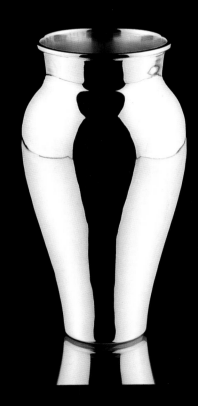

96

TEOTIHUACAN FLOWER VASE
FLORERO TEOTIHUACANO
fine silver .925 / *plata fina .925*

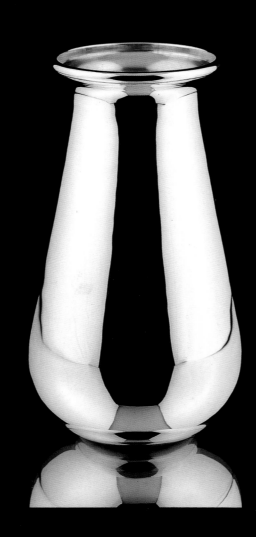

TARASCA JAR WITH CONCAVE NECK
JARRA TARASCA CON CUELLO CÓNCAVO
fine silver .925 / *plata fina .925*

98

**LARGE JAR WITH
POLYCHROMATED DRAIN**
*JARRÓN CON VERTEDERA
POLÍCROMO*
fine silver .925 / *plata fina .925*

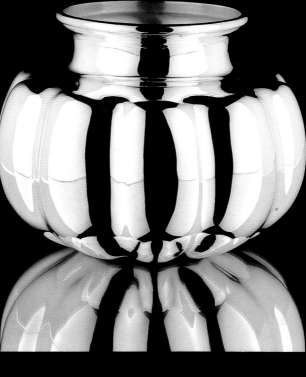

99

ORANGE GLOBULAR JAR
*JARRA ANARANJADA
GLOBULAR*
fine silver .925 / *plata fina .925*

100

**MIXTEC POLYCHROMATED
VESSEL**
*VASIJA POLICROMADA
MIXTECA*
fine silver .925 / *plata fina .925*

101

**TEOTIHUACAN ALABASTER
CONTAINER
*CONTENEDOR DE ALABASTRO
TEOTIHUACANO***
fine silver .925 / *plata fina .925*

102

SNAIL
CARACOL
fine silver .925 / *plata fina .925*

List of Photographic illustrations

CONTEMPORARY ART / ARTE CONTEMPORANEO

1. **SATURNINO HERRÁN**
Self-portrait / *Autorretrato*
undated / *sin fecha*
oil on canvas / *óleo sobre tela*

2. **SATURNINO HERRÁN**
Old Man's Head / *Cabeza de viejo*
undated / *sin fecha*
oil on canvas / *óleo sobre tela*

3. **SATURNINO HERRÁN**
The Offering / *La ofrenda*
undated / *sin fecha*
pencil on paper / *lápiz sobre papel*

4. **FRANCISCO GOITIA**
Self-portrait / *Autorretrato*
undated / *sin fecha*
oil on canvas / *óleo sobre tela*

5. **JOAQUÍN CLAUSELL**
Seascape / *Marina*
undated / *sin fecha*
oil on canvas / *óleo sobre tela*

6. **ROSARIO CABRERA**
The Girl with Pink Ribbon / *La niña con moño rosa*
undated / *sin fecha*
oil on canvas / *óleo sobre tela*

7. **ROSARIO CABRERA**
The Green-Eyed Lady / *La dama de los ojos verdes*
undated / *sin fecha*
oil on canvas / *óleo sobre tela*

8. **GERARDO MURILLO "DR. ATL"**
Volcanoes and Horizons / *Volcanes y horizontes*
1935
mixed media on playwood / *técnica mixta sobre triplay*

9. **GERARDO MURILLO "DR. ATL"**
The Popocatepetl Volcano / *El Volcan Popocatepetl*
1947
mixed media on dry-mounting / *técnica mixta sobre fibracel*

10. **DIEGO RIVERA**
Portrait of Juanita / *Retrato de Juanita*
1935
tempera on linen / *tempera sobre lino*

11. **DIEGO RIVERA**
Children Having Lunch / *Niños almorzando*
1935
oil on dry-mounting / *óleo sobre fibracel*

12. **DAVID ALFARO SIQUEIROS**
Giving of Toys / *Entrega de Juguetes*
1961
oil on wood / *óleo sobre madera*

13. **JOSÉ CLEMENTE OROZCO**
War Criminals / *Criminales de Guerra*
undated / *sin fecha*
oil on canvas / *óleo sobre tela*

14. **JOSÉ CHÁVEZ MORADO**
The Bricklayer / *El Adobero*
1980
oil on canvas / *óleo sobre tela*

15. **JOSÉ CHÁVEZ MORADO**
Tolteca
1961
oil on canvas / *óleo sobre tela*

16. **MANUEL RODRÍGUEZ LOZANO**
Woman Holding a Child / *Mujer con niño en brazos*
1927
oil on board / *óleo sobre tabla*

17. **PABLO O'HIGGINS**
Ramón Gómez Varela
1960
oil on canvas / *óleo sobre tela*

18. **ROBERTO MONTENEGRO**
Child with Parrot / *Niño con periquito*
undated / *sin fecha*
oil on canvas / *óleo sobre tela*

19. **ROBERTO MONTENEGRO**
The Green Apple / *La manzana verde*
1964
oil on masonite / *óleo sobre mansonite*

20. **FEDERICO CANTÚ**
God the Father / *Dios Padre*
1965
oil on canvas / *óleo sobre tela*

21. **FEDERICO CANTÚ**
Cana's Wedding / *Las Bodas de Caná*
1951
oil on canvas / *óleo sobre tela*

22. **EMILIO BAZ Y VIAUD**
Mexican Indian / *India mexicana*
1939
gouache and watercolor / *gouache y acuarela cartón*

23. **MIGUEL COVARRUBIAS**
Balinesa
undated / *sin fecha*
oil on canvas / *óleo sobre tela*

24. **RAÚL ANGUIANO**
Yalalteca
1977
oil on canvas / *óleo sobre tela*

25. **MARÍA IZQUIERDO**
Girls with Watermelon / *Niñas con sandía*
1946
oil on canvas / *óleo sobre tela*

26. **MARÍA IZQUIERDO**
Girl with Red Hat / *Niña con sombrero rojo*
1942
oil on canvas / *óleo sobre tela*

27. **FRIDA KAHLO**
Portrait of Isolda Pinedo Kahlo / *Retrato de Isolda Pinedo Kahlo*
1929
oil on canvas / *óleo sobre tela*

28. **FRIDA KAHLO**
My Dress hangs here / *Mi vestido cuelga aquí*
1933
oil and collage masonite / *óleo y collage masonite*

29. **GUNTHER GERZSO**
Blue Planes / *Planos en Azul*
1965
oil on dry-mounting / *óleo sobre fibracel*

30. **RAFAEL CORONEL**
Christ / *Cristo*
1956
oil on canvas / *óleo sobre tela*

31. **RAFAEL CORONEL**
The Herb Vendor / *El Yerbero*
1973
oil on canvas / *óleo sobre tela*

32. **RAFAEL CORONEL**
Child with Baby Doll / *Niño con Muñeca*
undated / *sin fecha*
oil on canvas / *óleo sobre tela*

33. **PEDRO CORONEL**
Celestial Navigators / *Navegantes celestes*
undated / *sin fecha*
oil on canvas / *óleo sobre tela*

34. **PEDRO CORONEL**
Head / *Cabeza*
undated / *sin fecha*
oil on canvas / *óleo sobre tela*

35. **PEDRO CORONEL**
Fantasy Corners II / *Rincones de ensueño II*
undated / *sin fecha*
oil on canvas / *óleo sobre tela*

36. **FRANCISCO CORZAS**
Portrait of Sandra / *Retrato de Sandra*
1978
oil on canvas / *óleo sobre tela*

37. **OLGA DONDÉ**
Quality of Life: Fig / *Calidad de vida, higo*
1974
oil on canvas / *óleo sobre tela*

38. **JESÚS REYES FERREIRA**
Christ in Three Parts / *Cristo en tres partes*
undated / *sin fecha*
gouache on paper / *gouache sobre papel*

POPULAR ART / *ARTE POPULAR*

39. JOSÉ ELOY RODRÍGUEZ VALENCIA
Blue Bridle with Silver Inlay / *Freno azul con incrustación de plata*
silver / *plata pavonada*
Amozoc de Mota, Pue.

40. SIMÓN CONTRERAS CAPILLA
Hand Basin / *Platón Palangana*
Talavera
San Pablo del Monte, Tlax.

41. TOMASA HERNÁNDEZ MARTÍNEZ
Red Huipil / *Huipil rojo*
waist weaving loom / *tejido en telar de cintura*
cotton textile / *textil en algodón*
San Pedro Amuzgos, Oax.

42. ROGELIO HERNÁNDEZ ANTONIO
Reed Water Car / *Carro pipa de carrizo natural*
sliced reed grass / *carrizo cortado y ensamblado*
San Juan Guelavia, Oax.

43. JOSÉ GARCÍA BAUTISTA
Bookcase / *Librero cómoda*
Engraved Zirimo Wood / *Madera de Zirimo ensamblada y grabada.*
Guanajuato, Mich.

44. MANUEL VALENCIA CHÁVEZ
Mask and Cap for the Black Dance
Máscara y gorra para danza de los negros
polychromated carved wood / *madera tallada policromada*
Sevina, Mich.

45. ELENA FELIPE FÉLIX
6 Pot Tower (Flowers and Birds)
Torre de 6 ollas (motivo flores y aves)
moulded and brunished clay / *barro modelado y bruñido*
Huancito, Mich.

46. BERNARDO MÁRQUEZ Y MADRIGAL
Vendor Couple / *Pareja de vendedores*
Panicua tejida
knited hard and soft fibers / *fibras duras y semi duras tejidas*
San Jerónimo, Purinchécuaro, Mich.

47. OSCAR GRANIZO TOVAR
Little Black Dance Horse / *Caballito de danza negro*
carved wood / *madera tallada*
Villas de San José, Cd. del Maíz, S.L.P.

48. LORENZO NARANJO E.
Wooden Indian Monkey / *Mono indio de madera*
polychromated and carved wood / *madera tallada y policromada*
Ejido San José, Cd. del Maíz, S.L.P.

49. CIPRIANO PÉREZ
Wooden Indian / *Indio de Madera*
polychromated and carved wood / *madera tallada y policromada*
Ejido San José, Cd. del Maíz, S.L.P.

50. MANUEL PÉREZ
Gorilla with Snake / *Gorila con víbora*
polychromated and carved wood / *madera tallada y policromada*
Ejido San José, Cd. del Maíz, S.L.P.

51. SEBASTIÁN GÓMEZ PÉREZ
Ceremonial Huipil / *Huipil Ceremonial*
waist weaving loom wool textile
textil en lana tejido en telar de cintura
Chacoma, Chiapas

52. ASUNCIÓN COBOS CRUZ
Three Musical Instrument Set / *Juego de tres instrumentos musicales*
assembled wood /
madera ensamblada
México, D.F.

53. JOSÉ ENRIQUE GALICIA FUENTES
Thirty Musical Instrument Set / *Juego de treinta instrumentos musicales*
jointed wood / *madera ensamblada*
Mexico, D.F.

54. ALFONSO CASTILLO ORTA
Mexico's Wealth (Tree of Life)
La riqueza de México (árbol de la vida)
moulded clay polychromated with natural tints
barro moldeado policromado con tintes naturales
Izucar de Matamoros, Pue.

55. REGINA REYNOSO THIELEN
The Mourning Virgen / *La Virgen de Dolores*
decorated glass / *vidrio decorado*
México, D.F.

56. RAÚL DE JESÚS ESPINOSA VÁZQUEZ
Fish / *Peces*
cedar carved wood / *madera de cedro tallada*
Papantla, Ver.

57. GILBERTO GONZÁLEZ CÓRDOVA
Top and "Valero" (Mexican Toy) / *Trompo y valero*
turned walnut tree wood / *madera de nogal torneada*
México, D.F.

58. FRANCISCO CORONEL NAVARRO
Large Sewing Box / *Costurero grande*
decorated lacquer with gold 23.5 K. / *laca decorada con oro de 23.5 K.*
Olinalá, Gro.

59. CELESTINO REZA MIJAREZ
Fiesta (Tabla Huichola)
yarn pressed on Campeche wax
estambre pegado con cera de Campeche
San Andrés Cohamiata, Jal.

60. INOCENCIA GONZÁLEZ
Willow Bark Skirt / *Falda de corteza de sauce*
knitted fibers (waist) / *tejido de fibras (cintura)*
Comunidad Cucapa, B.C.

61. INOCENCIA GONZÁLEZ
Pectoral
beaded macrame / *macramé con chaquira*
Comunidad Cucapa, B.C.

62. FLORENTINA LÓPEZ DE JESÚS
Brocaded Huipil / *Huipil Brocado*
waist loom brocade (textile cotton)
brocado en telar de cintura (textil algodón)
Xochistlahuaca, Gro.

63. SOFÍA FERRER GONZÁLEZ
Mazahua Doll / *Muñeca mazahua*
stuffed cloth / *trapo recortado y relleno*
San Felipe Santiago, Edo. de Mex.

64. EFRAÍN ROMERO SALINAS
Jorongo
pedal weaving loom / *tejido en telar de pedal*
Xonacatlán, Edo. de Mex.

65. PEDRO CELESTINO CELIS
The Nine Angels' Respect and Promise
El respeto y la promesa de los nueve angeles
brush drawing on bark / *dibujo a pincel en papel amate*
Xalitla, Gro.

66. MAGDIEL GARCÍA HERNÁNDEZ
Decorated Bottle with Mexican Eagles
Botella decorada con águilas mexicanas
engraved glass / *vidrio grabado con punta*
México, D.F.

67. JOSÉ LUIS GRANIZO TOVAR
King Mask / *Máscara Rey*
carved wood / *madera tallada*
Villas de San José, Cd. del Maíz, S.L.P.

68. FORTUNATO HERNÁNDEZ BAZÁN
Colored Agave Net / *Red de pita de colores*
knitted agave hard and soft fibers / *pita tejida en macramé*
(fibras duras y semiduras)
San Pedro Cajonos, Oax.

69. IRMA CANSECO MORGAN
Pitcher Lamp / *Cántaro lámpara*
black moulded and latticed clay / *barro negro modelado y calado*
San Bartolo Coyotepec, Oax.

70. IRMA GARCÍA REYES
Seven Leaf Set / *Juego de siete hojas*
tissue paper cutout / *papel de china picado*
Papantla, Ver.

71. BENITA MARTÍNEZ RUIZ
Doll Bell / *Campana muñeca*
moulded decorated clay
barro modelado y decorado al pastillaje
San Miguel Aguascalientes, Ver.

72. ADOLFO Y ABEL DOMÍNGUEZ SÁINZ
Eagle Devouring a Snake
Aguila devorando una serpiente
carved wood / *madera de calabozo tallada*
Alto Lucero, Ver.

73. LA TRINIDAD
Undulated Fruit Dish / *Frutero de ondas*
majolica and talavera / *mayólica y talavera*
Puebla, Pue.

74. OLIVER VELÁZQUEZ SERRANO
Hispanic Native Drum / *Tambor autóctono hispánico*
carved wood / *madera tallada*
Suchiapa, Chis.

75. LEYDI JIMÉNEZ BOJORQUEZ
Virgin of Guadalupe's Guild Banner
Estandarte de Gremio Virgen de Guadalupe
embroidery / *bordado con hilo iris*
Mani, Yuc.

76. LEONEL SALAZAR MARRUJO
The Patron Saint of Iztapalapa
El Santo Patrono de Iztapalapa
papier maché / *papel maché*
México, D.F.

77. TITO RUTILO CIPRIANO
Daily Life / *La vida diaria*
painted papier maché / *papel maché pintado*
Xalitla, Gro.

78. FRUCTUOSO ZALAPA LUNA
Seventh Guitar / *Guitarra séptima*
assembled wood / *madera ensamblada*
México, D.F.

79. INOCENTE CASTILLO DEL AGUILA
Four Cazuela Set / *Juego de cuatro cazuelas*
moulded clay / *barro moldeado*
Metepec, Edo. de Mex.

80. JERÓNIMO LÓPEZ MÉNDEZ
Bullskin Mask / *Máscara de piel de toro*
folded and sewed bullskin / *piel de toro doblada y cosida*
Col. San Marcos, Ocosingo, Chis.

81. ARTURO ESTRADA Y CIRILA GONZÁLEZ
Silk Reboso / *Reboso de seda*
waist loom / *telar de cintura*
Santa María del Río, S.L.P.

82. FRANCISCA POSAR QUIRÓZ
Skeleton Horse / *Caballo esqueleto*
moulded, polychromated and lacquered clay
barro modelado, policromado y laqueado
Ocumicho, Mich.

83. JOSÉ LUIS CERDA BÁEZ
Three Piece Dish and Bowl Cupboard
Trastero tinajero de 3 piezas
carved wood / *madera tallada*
Pátzcuaro, Mich.

84. JUSTA MATEO CRUZ
Pichancha
moulded and latticed clay / *barro modelado y calado*
San Marcos Tlapazola, Oax.

85. HIPÓLITO LÓPEZ ORTEGA
Farriswheel / *Rueda de la Fortuna*
carved and painted wood / *madera tallada y pintada*
San Martín Tilcajete, Oax.

86. GLORIA MENDOZA LUIS
Fine Girdle / *Faja fina*
waist weaving loom / *tejido en telar de cintura*
Santo Tomás Jalietza, Oax.

87. ISAÍ VERA CARRILLO
Tray / *Bandeja*
moulded and polished clay / *barro modelado y bruñido*
Los Reyes Metzontla, Pue.

88. MARÍA CARMEN PULIDO
Jewelry Box / *Alhajero*
carved wood / *madera tallada*
Apaseo el Alto, Gto.

89. PEDRO JIMÉNEZ ANZUETO
Tenderness (Lacandon boy with spider monkey)
Ternura (niño lacandón con mono araña)
one piece carved wood / *madera tallada a una sola pieza*
Chiapa de Corzo, Chis.

90. MARÍA ANTONIA PÉREZ HERNÁNDEZ
Camarín
lacquer decorated with oil / *laca fondeada y decorada al óleo*
Chiapa de Corzo, Chis.

91. OLMEC CENTER
CENTRO OLMECA
fine silver .925 / *plata fina .925*

92. GUAJE OLINALÁ
fine silver .925 / *plata fina .925*

93. **JALISCO JAR**
JARRA JALISCO
fine silver .925 / *plata fina .925*

94. **TRIPOD VESSEL FROM XOLALPAN CHICO'S**
VASIJA TRÍPODE DE XOLALPAN CHICO
fine silver .925 / *plata fina .925*

95. **MAYAN TRIPOD BOWL**
CAJETE TRÍPODE MAYA
fine silver .925 / *plata fina .925*

96. **TEOTIHUACAN FLOWER VASE**
FLORERO TEOTIHUACANO
fine silver .925 / *plata fina .925*

97. **TARASCA JAR WITH CONCAVE NECK**
JARRA TARASCA CON CUELLO CÓNCAVO
fine silver .925 / *plata fina .925*

98. **LARGE JAR WITH POLYCHROMATED DRAIN**
JARRÓN CON VERTEDERA POLÍCROMO
fine silver .925 / *plata fina .925*

99. **ORANGE GLOBULAR JAR**
JARRA ANARANJADA GLOBULAR
fine silver .925 / *plata fina .925*

100. **MIXTEC POLYCHROMATED VESSEL**
VASIJA POLICROMADA MIXTECA
fine silver .925 / *plata fina .925*

101. **TEOTIHUACAN ALABASTER CONTAINER**
CONTENEDOR DE ALABASTRO TEOTIHUACANO
fine silver .925 / *plata fina .925*

102. **SNAIL**
CARACOL
fine silver .925 / *plata fina .925*

Produced by
AFAN GRAFICO, S.A.
Madrid - Spain

Project Director
MATEO MAZAL BEJA, Esq.
Vice-President of Pulsar Internacional

General Coordinator
GREGORIO PUENTE CARBAJO

Fhotography
AGUSTIN GARCIA
Monterrey, N.L., México

Graphic Design
ASESORIA Y SERVICIOS EN IMAGEN, S.A. DE C.V.
Monterrey, NL - México

Style Editor
Prof. RICARDO TORRES MARTINEZ

Produced, Printed and bound by
AFAN GRAFICO, S.A. - TORREANGULO ARTE GRAFICO, S.A.
Madrid - Spain

Exhibition Curators
CARLOS A. VELAZQUEZ MORENO, Architect
Ms. CONSUELO FERNÁNDEZ RUÍZ

Museographers
CARLOS A. VELAZQUEZ MORENO, Architect
PEDRO MORUA ALONSO, Architect

produced on june 29, 1995,
by Afán Gráfico, S.A.-Torreangulo, S.A.
First printing 3.000 copies. Bound in teflex.
Printed on semi-gloss 100 Lb. paper
with achromatic PCR color selection.